Never Forsaken

Never Forsaken
Bishop Ted G. Thomas Sr.

New Community Temple Church of God in Christ

2017

Copyright © 2017 by Bishop Ted G. Thomas Sr.

All rights reserved. This book or any portion thereof may not be reproduced or used in any manner whatsoever without the express written permission of the author or the publisher except for the use of brief quotations in a book review or scholarly journal.

First Printing: 2017

All scriptures are quoted from the King James Version

ISBN: 978-0-9989163-8-5

New Community Temple Church of God in Christ
3615 Tyre Neck Road
Portsmouth, VA 23703
www.nctcogic.org
757.484.8903

Editors:
M. Dayan Araujo
Distronya M. Harris
Mother Charletta Thomas

Cover by: Tracey's Touch

Ordering Information: Special discounts are available on quantity purchases by corporations, associations, educators, and others. For details, contact the New Community Temple Church of God in Christ at the above-listed address.

U.S. trade bookstores and wholesalers: Please contact: New Community Temple COGIC

DEDICATION

This book is dedicated to my lovely wife, Charletta and to the memory of my mother Nancy Thomas and my father, Simuel Thomas Sr. To my sons, Ted Jr., Chris, Marc, Charles, Jonathan and Rueben and all nine of my grandchildren: Charles (CJ), Emanuel (Eman), Marc Jr. (MJ), Kiara, Evan, Aaron, Ted Junious (TJ), Naami and Marson.

My parents Elder Simuel and Mother Nancy Thomas

ACKNOWLEDGEMENTS

To my wife, Charletta, thank you for sharing nearly sixty years of your life with me. I'm glad we took this journey together.

To my sons, Ted Jr., Marc, Chris, Charles, Jonathan and Reuben and their wives, thanks for your love and continued support, whether big or small, it means a lot to me. I'm proud of you.

To my grandchildren, thank you for bringing so much joy to my life. I am expecting great accomplishments from each of you.

To the members of St. Stephens Church of God in Christ, in Virginia Beach and New Community Temple Church of God in Christ in Portsmouth, Virginia, thank you for trusting me to preach the gospel and allowing me to lead you.

To the Pastors and Members that compose the greatest Jurisdiction in the Church of God in Christ, The First Ecclesiastical Jurisdiction of Virginia. Thank you very much for all your love and support thirty-two years and counting.

CONTENTS

DEDICATION v
ACKNOWLEDGEMENTS vii
CONTENTS ix
FOREWORD xi
ENDORSEMENT xvii
INTRODUCTION 1
Chapter 1: God in the Country 7
Chapter 2: The Value of Education 17
Chapter 3: The Big City 25
Chapter 4: A Call to Preach 33
Chapter 5: Meeting Charletta Clifton 41
Chapter 7: Chosen to Be a Leader 53
Chapter 8: By His Stripes 59
Chapter 9: Spreading the Gospel 67
Chapter 10: Count up the Cost 71
CONCLUSION 81

FOREWORD

Consider the ancient British herald, Cometh the man cometh the moment. The thought of Bishop Ted Thomas is illustrative of what some theologians call chairos time, spiritually defined and preserved seasons. Indeed, he is now, but he has not always been an esteemed patriarch in the faith. From his early days as a cotton picker in his native North Carolina until his rise to community leader, bank executive, mathematician, educator, great-great grandfather

... what an amazing journey!

From meager beginnings and labor in the post office, he has risen to the splendid heights of consecrated bishop in one of the most historic COGIC jurisdictions, an ecclesiastical judge, and a distinguished one of THE 12 on the apostolic general board of the flagship holiness-Pentecostal denomination in North America. Rarely does one find such a human canvas of four score years with so much to admire and so much to learn and so much wonderment left over. This is a chairos season for us and for the bishop.

Perhaps I have uniquely benefited from my deceased mother's birth and family ties to Portsmouth-Norfolk, Virginia. The long time "state mother" of Virginia, Mother Beulah Dabney, was a near kinswoman to mother's family. Such maternal associations have provided one of my pinnacle privileges. I had the privilege (from a distance and first hand) to observe and probe portions of the sojourn of Bishop Ted Thomas. Several of these destiny intersections are chronicled in this book. Visiting his environment, preaching where he pastors, working together in the Board of Bishops and the General Assembly, charting COGIC Virginia history together, critiquing education and cultural shifts, and knowing his family —my personal enrichment.

Several historical markers exhibit personality contrasts so profusely telling until most of his comrades and disciples find themselves in suspended amazement. Ted Thomas was not born into ecclesiastical royalty; his wife was. The Clifton and Cypress families were legendary in his adopted state of Virginia. Most of his Negro fellows of the 1940's and early 50's were considered respectable if they graduated from a segregated high school. Ted Thomas did so, but also completed college and a graduate degree while raising a family, working full time and launching his pastoral ministry.

Once his denominational diocese encountered severe potential tensions and many of his clergy peers fled to tranquil and attractive ecclesiastical seas. Ted Thomas vowed, as a matter of ethical and spiritual principal, to support and assist Bishop David Love and his diocese until righteousness prevailed among the saints. Then, he sent two of his biological sons to an experimental re-activated private high school in

Mississippi, staking his claim and trust in the benefits of Christian, black, holistic education. Bishop Thomas exampled the lip service posited by others for others. And in the last decade, he led the building of two church edifices in Portsmouth and Virginia Beach while conjoining entrepreneurship and community empowerment. Also, he successfully insisted on integrating cultural and Christian authenticity for African-Americans and Christians. How does a black man muster the wherewithal to accomplish so much so well?

This readable and inspiring saga is clearly the record of a man with faith in his God, hard work in his nature and confidence in his divinely given potential and calling. When most men are reaching for the rocking chair, newest golf course, chilling with the fruit of their labor, or turning into an aging, bitter, bore . . . Bishop Ted Thomas is continuously gearing up for the next chapter of his life-book. To reference the vernacular of our tradition, he is "filled with the

Holy Ghost and a mighty burning fire." He has as much blazing holy fire in his bones as when he first told God "yes." Now, one of the few remaining sages in our church humbly allows us to visualize the message others have merely mouthed. Though 20 years my senior, his fatherly wisdom and practical expertise classify him as a MUST HAVE for my ministry and our era. Never Forsaken is as much a beacon for your future as a testimony of the Ted Thomas past. As you read these simple but compelling pages, be blessed by captions of a sainted father who has lived the gospel of holiness. More importantly, he is yet living the Gospel promise for each of us, . . . He will never forsake you . . .

Bishop LF Thuston, M.A, M.Div., Th.D.
Chairman - General Assembly
Church Of God In Christ, Inc.

ENDORSEMENT

My dad, Bishop Ted Thomas is a man of integrity, great wisdom, strength, and perseverance. These are more than words; they are true. I watched how when we were building St. Stephens Church of God in Christ in Virginia, Beach Virginia. He was older at the time, but he did not just watch us build. He helped to build with us. He showed us what to do and how to do it.

My dad is not a standoffish leader. He helps anyone; He is down to earth. He loves people, and he loves the church. I still remember how he handled his loss on the General Board. He has been elected twice since that time, but I observed how he kept supporting the Church of God in Christ, despite the loss. He kept loving the church.

I admire how my dad put God over everything. He loves his family, and he takes care of us. If there is anything we need he helps us to get it, but he puts

God above us. He believes if God is the head of everything, then everything will fall into place. I have watched it work for him, and so I apply it to my life.

Reuben Thomas
Youngest son of
Bishop Ted G. Thomas Sr.

PREFACE

Society has trained us to look for God in the materialistic possessions so whenever we are surrounded by lack, we tend to overlook God's provisions. We become bombarded with issues, and we do not see God's personal concern for us.

One way to see God is by assessing our journeys and asking ourselves how did we make it this far? How did we survive our hardships? We could attain nothing without God supplying our needs. We could get nowhere without God's guidance, and we would not be alive today without God's safety. God protects us, and God provides. Even through tough times, the wisdom and strategy God gives, help us get from one situation and problem to the next. God has promised that He will never leave nor forsake His children. I am a personal witness He can keep you if you want to be kept. He will supply every one of your needs. He will uplift you when your head hangs low.

David in Psalm 37:25, said: "I once was young, and now I am old yet have I never seen the righteous forsaken nor his seed begging bread." I can tell you I feel the same way. Here I am over eighty years old, and I can still testify that God has never forsaken me. For each phase of my life, God stayed with me and provided for me. Because I was faithful to Him, He multiplied everything I had.

I sought Him, and He supplied me with all I needed. God is my source. He is my sustainer. I have no reason to fear.

-Bishop Ted G. Thomas Sr.

INTRODUCTION

I was a country boy, born in 1935, in Roberson County, North Carolina. My family moved to Hoke County, a rural area, called Bowmore, North Carolina, about five miles west of Raeford when I was of school age. I grew up there until I was seven years old. My father was a farmer, and my mother was a homemaker. We were a poor black family living in the South but my parents never told me that we were poor; and I never considered myself as being poor.

My mother had ten children, seven lived and three died at childbirth. I was the seventh of my siblings to be born. From the time I can remember, I shared in the work on the farm. Even as a toddler, I picked cotton and later learned how to plow and work in the field. In those days on the farm, children were a resource. The boys had to help with the farming and feed the animals while the girls cooked, washed clothes, and cleaned the house plus worked on the farm. Everybody worked. We all had to pitch in and pull our weight. I was the seventh of my siblings but as I grew older, I watched how babies were carried to the field and slept while the family picked cotton. When they became old enough to walk, they also learned to pick cotton.

At a young age, I learned how to cook. I would pick turnips and collard greens; get the worms off them; take each leaf and place it in salt water with a pinch of washing powder to clean them real good; rinse them three times. Sit the greens in the sink to let them drain. Cut up the greens and put them in the pot with about four cups of water. I washed a piece of ham hock and then add it to the greens as seasoning meat. I learned not to cook them too long or they would be mushy. I trained myself to go by the taste; I waited until they were soft and tender. My mother made sure her children knew how to survive.

I grew up in a saved home and I had good solid parents. My mother was a praying woman. She was serious about her relationship with God and she loved the church. She was a stickler for doing right and would always tell us to live holy. She taught us, don't say you're living holy, and you're not living holy; if you say you're going to live right then live right. She did not tolerate any hypocrisy.

My father was a quiet person. He was more of a doer than he was a talker. He was a preacher; he went to church and supported the church. He brought his money home, and he took care of his family. My father didn't engage in a lot of unnecessary talks. He would say, "Don't talk too much; folk don't know what you know." When we did wrong, he would tell us what we did wrong, and he was done.

My father always taught us to work hard, keep a roof over your family's head and keep food on the table. You may have to let go of some other things but take care of the necessities. Because of my father, we always had a place to live. We were never without lights and we always had food to eat; it may not have been what we wanted but we had something to eat.

We had a good family. As children, my siblings and I did not get into much mischief or fights. We were taught to not do wrong. There was one time when my siblings and I were being messed with on the way home from school. My oldest brother wanted to retaliate but didn't really know what to do. He ran all the way home and grabbed the shot gun my dad used to go hunting. Then he ran all the way back to the very spot where the guys were teasing us. By the time he got back the boys were gone. He was confused and frustrated. I just watched him. Even I knew, you can fire a shotgun from a distance but it was obvious, he did not know what he was doing. It was because my parents did not raise us to be vengeful or violent.

From as long as I can remember, God carried us from season to season. When my family should have starved in the winter, God provided for us. When we were held back as a family, God provided us a way out. When we should have settled, God guided us and gave us new direction and opened new doors. God was the strategy of wisdom that carried my family through the tough times.

Well children, times have changed and nothing is forever. But, I pen this written record that I sought to please the Lord and I loved Him with all my heart. Through this book, I encourage and admonish you to genuinely seek the righteousness of God in all that you do. I have been faithful to God and He has never forsaken me. If you trust Him, He will do the same in your life.

Never Forsaken

Chapter 1: God in the Country

It is said, if you want to know the true character of a person observe how they respond during difficult times. I became acquainted with the essence of who my parents were, by watching how they lived in the country of North Carolina. They were examples of true vision and strong character.

When we lived in the country, we did not have electricity. Light poles were not installed in Hoke County until around the mid-1940s, so we lived with lamp lights fueled by kerosene. We studied our school lessons using lamp lights. The lamp lights had shades that were clear glass, shielding the glare of the light. Another responsibility of the boys was to clean the lamp shade each night so we could study.

We didn't have running water. Our water came from out of the ground. To draw the water, we had a pump on the porch that was attached to a long pipe that went down until it hit water. We had to prime the pump in order to pull the water up into a bucket. That is how we got our water.

Through all our lack, my parents trained our eyes to see the riches of what we possessed, which was God and family.

Life in the country was intentional. We did not waste our time or our resources. We were farmers, which required us to be planners. We had to plant in the spring or we would starve in the winter! We grew just about all our food: sugar canes, watermelon, cotton, corn, peanuts, wheat, collard greens, Crowder peas, fields peas and any kind of bean you can think of: navy beans, butter beans, red beans, black beans, pinto beans, you name it we raised it.

We also ate every bean we raised. My mother cooked beans often but she never had to worry about our appetite. Because we toiled and worked hard out in the field, we were ravenous when it was time to eat.

Bishop Ted G. Thomas Sr.

We did not turn down food. We either ate whatever was placed before us or we went to bed hungry; those were our options. I loved to eat cooked Crowder peas but I did not like pinto beans. When my mother cooked Crowder peas, I'd eat until my heart was content but if I saw that my mother had cooked those big, thick, brown pinto beans, I would go to bed hungry that night. I refused to eat them and my mother was content with letting me go to bed hungry. We had to respect our provisions.

We made our own molasses and canned tomatoes, peaches, and sauerkraut in mason jars during the summer so we could have food in the winter. I would watch how we had to carefully store these vegetables and fruits! One of my chores included helping to prepare tomatoes for canning! I observed the way tomatoes required special attention. For example, my mother had to leave the lids loose on the jars or the gas from the acid in the tomatoes would cause the jars to burst! We couldn't waste the mason jars or the tomatoes. We planned for the future!

During that time, we did not have refrigerators. We had what was called an ice box. We would go to town on Saturdays and purchase a 50-pound block of ice, carry it home, and placed it at the top of the ice box to preserve our food as well as keep our fresh dairy products, ice cream, and any other desired and other perishable food fresh. That 50-pound block of ice would keep our food and beverages cold for several days.

My father was the epitome of a true provider and he did the best he could to take care of his family. He was a hard worker and always provided for us. He taught us to always keep a roof over our head and food on the table. A skilled hunter, he killed squirrels, rabbits, raccoons (we called coons) and more. There were days we didn't know where our next meal was coming from, but God would allow my dad to go hunting and we would have rabbit for supper. My dad would kill it, skin it and clean it, then my mom cooked it and we had a meal.

My father would kill hogs during the winter and cured the pork with salt to preserve it. Salt came as a solid square block either ten or twenty pounds each. My father would rub the pork down with the salt. Pork was probably our main meat. I think back now and understand why high blood pressure was so prevalent in our community; it is because salted meat was frequently included in our diet. We raised and preserved just about everything we ate.

From watching my family cure meat, I grasped the significance and impact of salt. Later, I clearly understood how the verse, "ye are the salt of the earth" applies to our everyday walk as believers.

In Matthew 5:13, Jesus said, *"Ye are the salt of the earth; but if the salt have lost his savour, wherewith shall it be salted? it is thenceforth good for nothing, but to be cast out, and to be trodden under foot of men".* I observed that salt has at least four uses:

First, salt is a preserver; we doused our meat with salt. It did not matter which meat it was or how large it was, the salt was able to preserve it. We relied on salt. If the salt had no strength, all that we worked for and hoped to carry us throughout the season would be wasted. As believers, our spiritual lives should be effective as salt. We become seasoned by focusing our attention on God, adhering to the Word of God and spending time with God. When we walk in the favor of God, our lives are effective. In Exodus 32:9, when God wanted to destroy the children of Israel because of their wickedness, Moses had a conversation with God that changed God's mind. Because of Moses' relationship and rapport with the Lord, God respected what Moses said to Him. In 1 Kings 11:13, when God was punishing Solomon, He said, *for my servant's David sake* I will not destroy the whole kingdom; I will leave one tribe. God preserved a portion of the kingdom because of David. Sometimes our faithfulness and our reputation with God has God protecting and surrounding those in our lives who would have ordinarily been destroyed. God preserves our families and generations because of us. In return, we should be making the difference in the world not conforming to it. Jesus said in Matthew 5:14, "Ye are the light of world." Our light should shine bright enough to light up in this dark world of sin.

Secondly, salt has the tendency to make one thirsty. After consuming salted meat, we needed water. We did not grab sodas, we thirsted for water. Jesus said in Matthew 5:6, *"those who hunger and thirst after righteousness shall be filled."* Saints of God should be so consumed with the righteousness of God until people who partake of our conversation, and share our company, start thirsting for God. They start seeking a deeper and better relationship with God. Before we can even invite them to our church, they'll ask us; they'll seek out our church. We must allow our flesh to decrease so that sinners who come around us start seeking for the Living Water. We as Christians should live so that men would see our good works and want to be like us and want what we have.

Next, salt has a healing ingredient in it. It is often used as a saline solution. As long as salt had strength, it could reduce soreness and drive out certain infections. Jesus said in Mark 16:18, *"in my name, shall you lay hands on the sick and they shall recover."* It's not our hands that heal but it's the healing power of God that does the work. God's spirit empowers us to do what we do. Walk honestly before God. When you know you're living for God, you shall lay hands on the sick and they shall recover.

Lastly, salt is used to season our food. As saints, the words we speak should be representative of the wise God we serve. Colossians 4:6 says, "Let your speech be always with grace, seasoned with salt, that you may know how you ought to answer every man." Our conversations should be wholesome. Our words should be seasoned with grace. Proverbs 25: 23 says, "... A word spoken in due season, how good is it!" We have been given the ministry of reconciliation (2 Corinthians 5:18). The words we speak should be used to build up, edify, and to add worth and significance to a person or situation; not to destroy lives.

I learned all of these uses of salt, as a young child growing up in the country and working on the farm with my family.

Because we were a poor family, we did not own our own farm. So, my father became a sharecropper. Under the sharecropping system, the land owner would allow you to work their land in exchange a portion of the profit from the harvest produced. Once my dad received one-third of the profit from the harvest, any money he had borrowed from the land owner for equipment and supplies, had to be paid back to the land owner. After reimbursing the land owner, there was very little left for my dad. The unfairness of the sharecropping system was intended to keep blacks in slavery.

My dad later moved the family from the white man's farm to a black man's farm but the struggle still existed. The owner looked white but he was black. My dad told my oldest brother and my other siblings to continue working on the black man's farm, while he worked for the government at Fort Bragg, in Fayetteville, North Carolina. Because so many men were leaving the farm life, the North Carolina state government passed a law requiring all men who worked on the farm to return to the farm to harvest the owner's crop. My dad said his boss had to lay him off because of that reason. From that time, my family over-emphasized the importance of education.

Chapter 2: The Value of Education

Each year, in North Carolina, blacks started school in mid-September after cotton-picking season was over. Whites did not have to worry about picking cotton, so they started school the last week of August. Once our school year began, our school years were shorter than whites because we had to go back to the farm to chop the cotton which involved getting the weeds and grass out of the cotton and preparing it to grow. School years started late in the Fall and ended early for us in the Spring.

Although my parents strongly emphasized the importance of education, we could not negate our household responsibilities. We had to take care of home and pursue our education. We learned balance. We had to live a balanced life.

On school mornings, my four brothers and I had to wake up early and feed the animals, milk the cows, and feed the hogs before walking between a quarter mile and a half mile to school. People talk about the old greasy bags, but we carried our lunches in brown bags that became greasy over time. We could not afford lunch pails so every day we used the same ole brown bag to hold our lunch which was ham between a piece of biscuit.

Schools were segregated as you can imagine. Whites and blacks did not attend school together. I do not recall if I ever saw the white students' school but our school was literally a house made up of four rooms. I still remember the principal of the school, Professor Campbell. He was a black Presbyterian who was kind and did all he could for the students. One of the rooms in the schoolhouse was used as a lunch room. I recall Professor Campbell putting water on an old pot belly stove, used to put moisture in the air during the winter time. Then he would place our hands over the pot belly stove to help warm them up from the cold walk to school. He cared about

Bishop Ted G. Thomas Sr.

educating us and he cared about us as people. Education was valued and we were eager to learn.

I was a good student at school but the one time I allowed myself to be influenced by peer pressure, it was as if God Himself was trying to teach me a lesson. I remember, I was in first grade, and one of my friends Daniel Ferguson, brought some "chewing tobacco" to school. We were the same age, about five or six years old, but Daniel was an experienced tobacco chewer; he knew how to chew the tobacco, how to hold it in his mouth and spit out the juice. One day, Daniel convinced me to go under the schoolhouse and chew some tobacco with him during lunch time. Well, I did. Just as I put the tobacco in my mouth, the principal came around the school and rang the bell for us to go back to class. I panicked.

Because I didn't know how to hold the tobacco in my mouth like Daniel, I swallowed it. I soon learned why Daniel never ate his tobacco and why he never swallowed his saliva. Immediately, my stomach started to toil and burn. I was in so much pain, the principal called my parents and my parents had to carry me home. I was sick for about three days. I couldn't go to school or do anything. My parents did not have to chastise me; the tobacco did it for them. Man, I never wanted to see tobacco ever again. At a young age, I learned my lesson about influence. From then on, I went to school and did what I was supposed to do. Any lesson that was taught at school, I was eager to learn it.

When I left the rural part of North Carolina and moved to Norfolk, Virginia, my passion for learning never stopped. I remember, while I was in school, in Norfolk County High, I would go with the teachers to the white schools and get their secondhand books and materials. When the white students got new books and new microscopes, we had to go to their schools and get their old books and damaged microscopes. Nevertheless, we learned. We were taught if you want to be something, go to school and get an education. Despite the condition of the books, we gained knowledge. Going to school meant something to us; we used school to prepare us for life. We went to school to be able to select the job we wanted and we knew what we wanted to do when we graduated.

I observe now how generations have passed and children do not understand the importance of education. They go to school with no idea what they would like to become when they finish. They go to college and require additional training after they are done. They have no chores; they have no responsibilities. Consequently, they have no appreciation for where they are. They seek to adopt what is new because it is convenient. The viewpoints of old are dismissed and old traditions are mocked but all my years have taught me, you do not abandon the past. If you abandon all of what has existed for what is new, then if what is new fails, you will either be stuck or forced to move but it will never be your choice. You will always have to rely on others to provide an alternative.

Because I obeyed and followed instructions at home and in the classroom, God used my education to open doors for me in the community and in the church. I have been blessed to establish businesses, sit on executive boards of businesses and banks, minister to congregations of diverse educational backgrounds, instruct students as a professor in universities and I still stand before the people of God to deliver the word of God. God can use you to reach more people in more places when you submit yourself to Him completely. If you want to go far in God, prepare yourself for where He wants to take you. Apply knowledge to your life by listening and receiving wisdom and instructions from the older generations who have it to give.

My parents lived without a formal education but I hold on to the way they taught my siblings and me

Bishop Ted G. Thomas Sr.

how to both live where we were and to prepare for the future. My family transitioned from the country life decades ago, but I still remember some of the lessons I learned while I was there. Some of the work I did in the country, I will never have to do again. It's not necessarily about the way we did things growing up but the principle behind what we did I still hold on to and cherish.

    I try to encourage the younger generations to learn from the past and hold on to their principles. God will carry you and make a way.

Never Forsaken

Chapter 3: The Big City

After the law was passed regarding men that were sharecroppers, my dad eventually moved to Norfolk, Virginia where one of his brothers and two of his sisters lived. Because he had previous experience working on the railroad, my dad was able to get a job with Norfolk Southern Railroad.

If you can imagine a country boy growing up in rural area with no electricity, no running water, no trucks, not many cars, and then moving to the city with bridges, cranes, lights, machinery and water, you can imagine my excitement when I first saw it all.

The city was exciting for me. I was easily amused and easily recognized differences around me. My family initially lived in a duplex when my father moved us to the Berkley section of Norfolk, Virginia. Berkley was a diverse community but mainly blacks lived there. I would often stay at my Aunt Bettie's home from time to time and once during the summer.

Aunt Bettie lived near the overpass of the railroad tracks. The trains passed underneath the overpass near her house and even that was fascinating.

The city was not the country. I could not maneuver my way around in the city like I could in the country. I remember when I was about nine years old, I attempted to walk home by myself. Somehow instead of going underneath the overpass, I walked over it. When I looked down and saw how high I had walked. Fear quickly raced through my body. Standing so many feet above houses, trains, and the ground, I did not know what to do. Paralyzed with fear, I dropped to my knees (not to pray) but to crawl down from off the overpass. My knees and hands were scratched, scraped, and bloodied but I refused to stand up and walk. When I made it back to my aunt's house, I never made the mistake of walking over the overpass again.

Bishop Ted G. Thomas Sr.

I loved my Aunt Bettie and I kept up with her. She was a leading member in her church. As long as I was at her house, I had to go to church every time she went, which was often. She placed me in the Bible Training Unit for young people and I had to participate. Growing up in the country my family went to a holiness church and after moving to Norfolk we attended the Ebenezer Church of God in Christ. The church styles were similar; they were both noisy and jubilant. But, my aunt attended the Mount Zion Baptist church in Berkley and going to a Baptist church was completely different. First, service was only an hour. I was used to being in church for three or four hours, in the holiness church, so it seemed like as soon as I sat down, in the Baptist church service was over. Secondly, it was quiet. To me, no one did anything. They didn't shout. They didn't dance. If someone got excited or happy an usher would run over to that person and spray something around their nose to make that person calm down. I didn't know what that spray was... I just called it "smelling salt."

Other than that, I did not mind spending time with my aunt.

My dad made pretty good money at Norfolk Southern Railroad so later on he moved the family to Crestwood in Norfolk County. We no longer had to work on the farm or pick cotton. In Crestwood, a vegetable man would come around the neighborhood selling vegetables, watermelon, collards, turnips, and we purchased our greens as he came through the streets. Despite this, my father maintained a garden of collard greens and turnips so we could always be self-sufficient. My father took care of the family and the household expenses.

My mother was a homemaker but sometimes she would go work on a truck farm. Back then Virginia had a lot of farms. There was a truck that picked us up and drove us to the farms in Prince Anne County, which is known today as Virginia Beach. We picked strawberries, spinach, radish, collards, green been, white potatoes, and more. Then, at the end of the shift the truck would drop us back off on our street. During the summer time when school was out, I would go with her.

I was about 15 years old, when my mother suffered from a slipped disc in her back. She experienced so much discomfort until she allowed the surgeons to operate on her back to repair the slipped disc. However, medical science was not as advanced during that time. When my mother left the hospital, she did not heal properly. She became ill again and was rushed back to the hospital where the doctors operated on her a second time.

This time when she came home fluid began to seep out of her back. She was bed-ridden for a while. My two sisters had moved back to North Carolina to aid my aunt who had also taken sick so it was up to my brothers and me to help with household chores. The missionaries from the church wanted to come by the house and help out but to respect my mother's privacy, I would not allow it. Learning responsibilities as a child proved beneficial throughout my mother's illness because I took over and I did what I refer to as the whole ball of wax. In other words, I did everything. I cooked, cleaned, washed dishes, washed clothes and took out the garbage the way my mother taught us.

The doctors wanted to operate on my mother a third time but she refused to go back because she said she allowed them to cut on her twice in one year and they did not correct the problem. I recall shortly afterwards, my family solicited prayers from the saints at the church. The people of God prayed. God heard them and the seeping from my mother's back stopped. God healed her.

Afterwards, I started working other jobs. While I was still in high school, my oldest brother, who was living in Washington, DC at the time, drove down in a new Cadillac convertible and then he allowed me to drive it to school. I was proud. I appreciated him for permitting me that car. My oldest brother looked out for me and I thought I was something.

If I wanted money, my father let me work for it. In eleventh and twelfth grade, after the school day ended, I worked at the telephone company in the cafeteria washing dishes and carrying out the garbage. I worked until about eleven o'clock at night. I also worked at the Canteen on the Norfolk Navy Base, a place where people socialized. My job was to make sandwiches. One summer, I worked for People Drugs Stores and more. I had worked my whole life but this time I was working for my benefit.

Years had passed. Once my siblings completed high school, they went to work; some got married. My oldest brother went into the service, but I worked and continued my education. I was the first in my immediate family to go to college and God's hands were guiding me to stay in Norfolk area all through life.

Chapter 4: A Call to Preach

I heard my dad testify of how God delivered him from drinking but by the time I was born, both of my parents had been converted. We always attended church. I have never known them to be unsaved.

In the country, many of my mother's side of family attended church with us so you can say we belonged to a family church. My mother was very active in the church and she played the piano. Our church would conduct annual fall revivals and whenever a revivalist came to town, my mother made space for them to stay in our home.

The presiding bishop, who lived in Salisbury, North Carolina, would come down often to conduct revivals. Whenever he visited, he would stay at our house. I carried his brief case before and after service. People then started telling me I was going to be a preacher. I was only about five years old, but I was faithful. I did not pay much attention to the fanfare; I just continued to serve. In the country, prayer service started at about 6:30 in the evening and ended around 8:00 p. m., then service would start. We would be in service until it ended around 11 o'clock at night.

We did not have television and not every family owned a radio so we had little distractions. We could take our time and learn how to live for the Lord. Line by line and verse by verse we were taught the scriptures so we knew what God required of us. People were stronger, more committed, and more consecrated because they took time to receive instructions.

I was taught in order to build a relationship with God, you must study His Word. The church taught us that God will provide and make a way, if we trust Him. When I heard that, I began to seek God and His guidance. From a child, the verse St. Matthew 6:33, "But seek ye first the Kingdom of God, and his righteousness; and all these things shall be added unto you" became real and became my favorite scripture. I would ask, what is the kingdom of God? And what are these things? No one could give me a satisfactory answer so I sought the Lord about it. Later, the Lord opened my understanding and revealed to me that the kingdom of God is righteousness, peace and joy in the Holy Ghost and these things are the material things of life that could be added. If I live by the principles of God, He will give me what I needed. As I grew older, I sought the Lord. I wanted to know His righteousness.

I recall my oldest brother, who became saved later in his life, took me to what we called a juke joint and brought me a beer; he tried to get me to drink it. My brother was like a father to me. I looked up to him and I loved to hang around him but I would not drink the beer he bought for me. I don't know why but I left him and the beer at the place and I went home.

My second oldest brother took me to Seaview Beach. It's where blacks would have parties and dances. Blacks were not permitted on Virginia Beach, except to work, so we went to Seaview Beach. When we got to the beach, music was playing on the juke box. My brother went out there and started doing the "grind" to Faye Adams' song, "Shake a hand, Shake a hand." While the music was playing, I left him too. He looked up and I was gone. I wanted to spend time with my older brothers but I was never satisfied in places like those. God would not allow it.

I did not hear a voice that called and say come go preach. I just had a burden in my spirit to do right and the only thing to satisfy that answer was to serve God. I do not recall resisting the voice of God. Instead, I found myself moving towards it. People always thought I was a preacher but I was a lay member. At a young age, I was saved. I worked in the church and I attended a lot of prayer meetings. I would go to early sunrise prayer service with my mother. When I was in high school, I had a friend that was also sanctified. We would leave school at lunch time to attend noon day prayer and then we had to rush back to school.

By the time I became a minister or preacher, I already knew how to seek the Lord and have a relationship with Him. I understood the righteousness of God is more important than meat and drink. It is more significant than positions or recognition. I accepted the position to carry on God's work. I preached my initial sermon in 1958 and although God blessed me to be promoted through the ranks in the church, seeking God's righteousness has always been my primary focus. Serving as a bishop in the Church of God in Christ, never shifted my focus off God or my attention from inquiring more about Him.

I later heard Bishop J. O. Patterson Sr. say something that resonated with me and I have never forgotten. Before his death in 1989, while addressing the Board of Bishops, he said, "You can add 'these things' to the righteousness of God but you cannot add God's righteousness to these things."

During his tenure as Presiding Prelate of the Churches of God in Christ, Bishop J. O. Patterson Sr. had spent much of his time traveling the country raising funds to build Saints Center (a vision that the Lord had given him for the Church Of God In Christ, Inc.) in Memphis, Tennessee. He tried to establish the Church of God in Christ College where he believed people would travel to attend because not many people would go to Mississippi for school. I understood Bishop Patterson's words to mean, had he gone around the country focusing more on the gospel and getting people saved, he could have raised the money for Saints Center. But because he focused on the work and raising the money, his efforts were not as successful. By the end of his life he had only broken ground but never built Saints Center.

Bishop Ted G. Thomas Sr.

Today, we still have many distractions. We have televisions, radios, phones and social media. We have so much to entertain us so we put God on a time limit. People want preachers to rush the service; they want preachers to show them specifically in the Bible where it says not to smoke or not to drink instead of sitting and being taught and learning the scriptures. As a result, they are not as strong as they could be; they struggle to believe God; they struggle to live saved; and they are not as consecrated as they should be.

Those who seek material things first, and think they can add the things of God to them are wrong; they are mistaken. You cannot add God to your materialistic agenda; you will not prosper. God must be the priority. We must put the righteousness of God first.

Never Forsaken

Chapter 5: Meeting Charletta Clifton

From the day I met Charletta Virginia Clifton, I was connected to her. I was drawn to her. I knew I wanted to marry her.

In the 1950s, my family had a singing group called the South Side Crusaders. I was the piano player for the group. One night we sung at a church in Portsmouth, Virginia and after singing I sat next to my oldest brother. Charletta came from out of the choir of the church and when I saw her walk, I said to my brother in a very deep voice, "The Lord is my shepherd. I see what I want." I kept watching her and my brother was telling me, "Man, go get her." Another guy had eyes for her but I went up there and got Charletta's number and I later called her.

We started talking and enjoying each other's friendship. I often say she was more saved than I was because during that time, it was considered a sin to go to the movies but I used to enjoy going to the movies.

Every Saturday, I would pay a nickel to go and watch a film. One time, I called myself taking her to the movies with me. She agreed to go with me but she could not get comfortable. She felt convicted the entire time. When we went down in that dark room and sat down she felt condemned. I tried to enjoy the movie but she kept squirming, jumping, and pinching my hand until I had to get up out of there. We left and I never looked back.

I started college while Charletta was still in high school. I was attending Norfolk State University, but I had to leave to go to Virginia State University to finish the last two years of college. By this time, we had developed affectionate feelings for each other. I was always concerned about living right. I read in 1 Corinthians 7:9, where it said it is better to marry than to burn. God instructed me, rather than sin, get married.

Bishop Ted G. Thomas Sr.

My college friends and I had our lives mapped out. We dreamed of the homes we would build but the Lord told me if I do right He would bless me with my dreams. In honor of God's word, I asked Charletta's dad, if I could marry her. I told my college roommates and they called me crazy.

I was the first of my mother's children to go to college, so telling my mother I was getting married was a big deal. I wrote my mother a long letter and shared the news. She responded in disappointment. She expressed her fear and displeasure of us getting married before finishing school. During that time, once people got married they did not finish school. They settled into married life and never looked back. My mother urged me not to marry but to finish school. I told her I was going to finish and I finished that semester.

On May 30, 1957, we got married. My mother was so devastated she did not attend the wedding. After we got married I worked at the post office and we rented a home. I started preaching the very next year and in 1959, God made a way that we had a brand-new brick house built from the ground up and we moved in it. A baby came along but Charletta went back to school and I went to school at night.

In 1960s, I was pastoring and going to school. Service started around 8:00 p. m. I would leave class and would walk into service at 8:30. At this point, I was taking courses every semester, without any breaks. More of my sons were born. My wife still managed to take care of the boys while I went to class at night.

When she started teaching, she brought the boys to my mother and I would come home from the post office and ensure dinner was prepared. We worked as a team and our parents watched us both finish college.

Bishop Ted G. Thomas Sr.

Yes, we struggled, but I enjoyed the teamwork. Some days it was tough to keep going, but we suffered through together. She never abandoned me. Instead, we built a partnership and worked together toward our goals. She didn't just sit on the sideline and watch me do; she was also active.

She never gave up on me; she always supported me and to this day, I continue to support her. I told her, I did not marry her for her to work in somebody's house. My encouragement was more than just words. I encouraged her to go back to school and when she went back, I did not change my mind. I supported her. I appreciated and cherished her commitment to me.

As I think back to our early years together, I know the key to us being successful in marriage for nearly 60 years is that we were equally yoked when we got married. Before we got married, we were both active in church. She was reared in the church her whole life; I was reared in church my whole life. She was already involved in church; I was already involved in church. She wanted to pursue her education; I wanted to pursue my education. We both enjoyed going to conventions. We both enjoyed youth conferences. We both had goals. I would have been in trouble if I wanted to go to church and she wanted to go to the dance hall. If I was involved in ministry and she was involved in something else, we would have had a problem. But we shared the same interests. We still have that love and enthusiasm for the church. If I encourage my wife to stay in and rest, and she stays, she thinks she has backslid.

Today, I see, how in too many cases, marriages are not working because their interests are too far apart. I encourage young people to first get their education, then ask the Lord to give them someone who is saved and compatible with them. You want someone who will stick with you and not abandon you when times get tough. Do not become unequally yoked. Church involvement is considered an interest. Education is considered an interest. A desire to be connected is an interest. I didn't try to marry someone unsaved first and then try to train her to be the way I wanted her to be. We talked a while and we made sure we were on the same page before we got married.

Throughout my entire marriage, I put God first and my marriage came second. I wanted to please God and God taught me how to please Him and how to please my wife. Even as a pastor, I am responsible for the spiritual well-being of the people and that is where it stops. As a husband, I have a responsibility to look after the physical well-being of my wife. God taught me how to always give the proper respect to the people of God and the proper respect owed to my wife.

I encourage you to desire a marriage God's way. God must be at the center of any marriage. You never can go wrong when you go with God because God cannot lie. When He says, He will give you the desires of your heart, He will. I have found Him to be true to every word and faithful to me, my wife and my family.

Mother Charletta Thomas

Chapter 6: Becoming a Father

After I married Mother Thomas, because of my obedience, God multiplied my name by blessing me with six healthy sons to ensure my lineage would continue. When my first son Ted Jr. was born, I was overjoyed. I had a good father so to know my first child was a son, meant a lot to me. My time was divided, but I trained him and kept him in church. I taught him as my father taught me. I taught him to take care of his family and to look after his mother.

After Ted Jr. was born, God didn't permit another child to be born to us for ten years. God divinely orchestrated time for me to become established. During that time, I was able to get on my feet and regain my bearing. I finished school and worked in the church. I also purchased my first home and completed more education. Afterwards, God allowed my next five sons to be born, Chris, Marc, Charles, Johnathan and Rueben. I knew God was smiling on me and giving me gifts from heaven. A mother's love is prevalent but I always wanted my sons to learn what a father's love felt like. I wanted them to know that their dad loved them too.

Attributes of my father and oldest brother helped to shape the parent I became. Apart from being a great provider, one quality I loved and admired about my father was his demonstration of confidence in me. I loved how he was an older person listening to a younger person; such level of attentiveness lets people know they are significant. Although I was still in school, my father would look to me for advice; he listened to what I had to say and he respected my judgement. My oldest brother always looked out for me. He would just do for me and give to me. He accepted me as me. I looked up to him and he allowed me to look up to him. The qualities of listening, demonstrating attentiveness, and showing concern and acceptance are qualities I hope my sons can say I demonstrated toward each one of them.

Bishop Ted G. Thomas Sr.

I believe if God gives you children then you should love your children. If God gave them to you then you should take care of them and provide for them, both sons and daughters. You don't restrain your love; you allow your love to flow. If children do not sense love from their parents, they will look for it in all the wrong places. I tried to demonstrate love and concern every day. I wanted my sons to know a father's love so they could express it to their children.

Never Forsaken

Chapter 7: Chosen to Be a Leader

The most difficult advice I ever had to give, came when I was about forty-nine years old. My father had been recently diagnosed with cancer and the doctors wanted to perform exploratory surgery to examine the extent of the disease. My father came to me and asked me what he should do. He did not show any sign of sickness but out of concern for my father, I advised him to take the practical route and have the surgery. After he was admitted into the hospital, I told him I was going to attend the Holy Convocation in Memphis, Tennessee. When the doctors cut him open to examine the extent of the cancer, they found that the cancer had metastasized and there was nothing they could do. However, the surgery had also hastened my father's condition and he died less than a week or two later, while I was at the Holy Convocation on Official Day.

I carried that burden in my heart for years. Had I not advised my father to have the surgery he could have lived weeks longer. Many times, I felt the reason he died sooner was my fault. I questioned time after time, why would my father trust my judgement? Why would he place his life in my hands? Why would he trust me to make a decision to determine if he would live or die? Many times, I personally felt I failed him.

Nonetheless, my father knew he was at the conclusion of his life. He knew it was his time to leave. By seeking my advice, he was in his own quiet way giving me the permission to become a leader and exercise judgment. I always looked up to my father and admired him but He was preparing me to become someone others looked up to and admired. In seeking my advice at this pivotal point of his life, my father was teaching me how to make decisions that would affect the well-being of other people. He was teaching me how to exercise vision. As leaders, we must make the decision to lead and to choose leaders.

Bishop Ted G. Thomas Sr.

At the beginning of Jesus' ministry, Jesus himself called each one of His disciples and told them to "follow me (Matthew 16:24)." He told them "take my yoke and learn of me (Matthew 11:29)". But as Jesus began transitioning His work on to His disciples, before He could die, Peter denied Him. Before He ascended, Thomas doubted Him and the other nine hid themselves from the people.

Jesus knew the insufficiencies of His disciples. However, after they had witnessed the resurrection of Christ and the power of the Holy Ghost, their lives, their ministries, and their convictions changed. The right encounter, in the right spirit, at the right time can change a person's life, ministry, and conviction. The right counsel can transform a person's way of thinking and way of living.

I often share of how when I first starting pastoring, I failed to delegate authority as soon as I could, when I was a young preacher. We had a small membership so I did a lot by myself. I drove the church bus to pick up the members for church. I played the piano. I sang in the choir. I preached the message and then I drove the members home. I did this because it had to be done. However, when God blessed me with men, I did not delegate. I continued to do everything on my own as if I needed to do so.

Years later, God directed me to Exodus 18:13-27. God through Jethro, Moses' father in law, taught Moses how to delegate authority. Jethro told Moses judging all the people and doing all the work is not good for him and He would not last long if he did not delegate authority. He told Moses to seek out able men, men with like spirit to handle the small cases while Moses handle the big cases. Moses took Jethro's advice and Jethro moved on.

As leaders, we must learn to select able men and allow them to work. We should groom them into becoming leaders and then let them lead. People are going to make mistakes as you give them work to do, but you must trust God and trust your teaching and let them work. God did not send us to stand in the way of their growth but to promote it.

In my life, I have very few regrets. I did my best with the resources God entrusted into my hands. If I had different resources, I imagine I would have made decisions based on those resources. However, I acknowledge one of my regrets is failing to delegate authority as a young preacher. Who knows how I could have empowered people to lead had I only trusted them.

My advice to any leader would be to first be humane. Love the people. Show love and concern toward them. Any leader ought to be approachable. Genuinely appreciate people and they will do whatever they can for you; they will appreciate you in return and buy-in to what you are doing.

Secondly, continue to improve yourself. Get educated. If you're going to pastor, you should have a formal training to meet the demands of the people. In today's congregation, the younger generations are going to college and becoming more and more educated. When you pursue educational accomplishments, you can speak their language and minister at their level.

Last but not least, delegate capable leaders to help carry out the work. Do not appoint people you cannot trust and do not overlook the people you can trust. Seek God's wisdom and strategy for putting someone in place and learn to delegate. If you don't learn soon, you'll burn out later.

Chapter 8: By His Stripes

For more than two decades, I had a broadcast I called, "Reflections of Faith." Each morning at ten o'clock, for fifteen minutes a day, I taught a bible lesson, prayed and permitted people to call in for prayer. I coined the phrase, "believe it and receive it." I made that statement every day on the broadcast.

Almost daily, people called in and testified of the miracles God had performed in their lives after I prayed for them. To keep them encouraged in the faith, I started writing newsletters which were also titled "Reflections of Faith", and I used it as a platform to recap some of the bible lessons I taught throughout the quarter. I began to receive names and addresses of subscribers and sent out the free publication throughout the Chesapeake, Virginia area. The newsletter contained encouraging words from my wife, church news and later Jurisdictional news. The people in the area became inspired.

Testimonies continued to pour in constantly. One Sunday morning, Mother Thelma Vaughn, drove about seventy miles south from Richmond, Virginia, where she lived to my church in Portsmouth to inform me that the doctors diagnosed her with breast cancer. She said as she prepared to go into surgery, God told her to come and ask me to pray for her. Out of obedience, she drove down and I prayed for her and she went back to Richmond. On the next day, she checked herself into the hospital. Before the doctors operated on her, they took another x-ray. This time, they found no cancer. God healed her and the cancer never came back for as long as she lived.

Sister Berenice Lane, a member of our church went with us one Wednesday night to Calvary Church of God in Christ, pastored by Elder Newby. We were preparing to close out service but she came up and asked for prayer. She told me she had to go to the hospital because the doctor told her she had breast cancer. I prayed for her on that night and when she went to the doctor's office, he took another x-ray and there was no cancer. She also lived years afterwards and it never returned.

When we preach faith, there will come a time when our faith will be tested. It does not matter how much we pray and lay hands on others and believe God for other people, the experience is different when the disease is in our own bodies. One day we, will have to have faith and a relationship with God to believe Him for ourselves. I believe the enemy said, "You've been praying for other people; now let me see what you are going to do when I afflict your body." Not long afterwards, he tried to put the disease of cancer on me.

One Saturday night, in 1988, I took sick. My body was in a lot of pain, so as a precaution, I drove to the emergency room. The doctors kept me overnight and performed test on me. On Sunday morning, the doctors entered the room and informed me I had lung cancer. The diagnosis came as a surprise because I was never a smoker. I did nothing that would lead to lung cancer. I believed it was a misdiagnosis but the doctors performed further test using sample tissues and x-rays and confirmed that I definitely had lung cancer. They informed me of the extent of the disease and that they would have to operate on me to take it out.

I left the hospital and went to church. I did not go into my secret closet. I stood in the pulpit and prayed out loud. Before I preached, I prayed and said, "Lord, I prayed for Mother Vaughn, you healed Mother Vaughn. I prayed for Sister Lane and you healed Sister Lane. Now Lord, heal my body!" And the Lord touched me and healed me. I felt the anointing of God stream through my body and I ran down the aisle and declared out loud and believed in my heart that God healed me.

Bishop Ted G. Thomas Sr.

The last week of May 1988, I went to the Hospital to set up a time for the operation and I told the doctors God healed me. I told them I would come back after I attended the International Women's Convention, but I am healed. The doctors doubted me and looked at me as if I were crazy. They wrote a letter and required me to sign it promising I would come back and if I did not return, the letter had a disclaimer that if I died, they were not liable.

I went to the International Women's Convention and checked into my hotel room. The room was filled with flowers my church congregation had sent me. I later told my congregation, "Y'all thought I was going to die looking at all those flowers, y'all sent me." I enjoyed the Women's Convention and on the Monday morning following the convention, I checked into Bayside Hospital, in Virginia Beach. God spoke to me and told me, "If you let them cut you I'll heal you back up." They placed tubes in my mouth and nose and they cut me open to operate.

When I woke up, about eight to ten doctors surrounded the bed. A nurse said, "They cut you open to handle your lungs; they pulled out the tubes." The doctors said, "We couldn't find cancer." The doctors apologized for cutting me open and they went away believing. Later that day, a delivery guy came in the recovery room. He stopped and looked at me. He continued to do his job but he would pause and look at me again. He said, "Mister, excuse me for looking at you, but it looked like you were dying on yesterday, and today you are sitting up."

God allowed each one of the testimonies people shared with me to strengthen my faith in Him and He carried me through. It is not doubt when you follow the doctor's instructions. Although, God told me He healed me, I followed doctor's orders and they left believing after they cut me opened. You can get a bad report and follow the doctor's orders but you deal with it by your faith... If you can believe it, Jesus can do what the doctors cannot do.

Bishop Ted G. Thomas Sr.

    I still believe in divine healing. I still know, if you can believe it, and don't doubt in your heart, you can receive it. I understand the power of God and the benefits of the cross. Before my sermons, I sing a song derived from Isaiah 53:3: *"He was wounded for our transgression, He was bruised for our iniquities. The chastisement of our peace was upon Him and with His stripes we were healed."* Jesus did not just save us. When they whipped Him, each stripe they put on Him was for our healing. If we have faith, and do not doubt in our hearts, any ailment we experience, God can take it away from us but the key is to not doubt in our hearts. We can say we believe but in our spirit we doubt and nothing happens for us. We can convince others with our mouth but yet we question God in our hearts and we receive nothing from God. Only believe. The Lord is a Healer! All things are possible if you only believe.

Never Forsaken

Chapter 9: Spreading the Gospel

I am an old-fashioned holiness preacher. I preach that holiness is a way of life. I know that if we accept the word of God as instructions for our lives, it will transform us. I have witnessed it time after time. A lot of times we want to try to fit God in our situations but God is too big and too wide. We must abide in Him and submit to His Word to be transformed. We must live by the Word. We must apply the word of God to our lives daily.

I often shared the story of how I was driving on I-264 East in Virginia Beach going to St. Stephen's Church of God in Christ where I pastor. While I was driving and Mother Thomas was sitting in the passenger seat, a young Caucasian male driver with several young Caucasian men in the car, came from behind my vehicle driving a high rate of speed. The driver got directly in front of my car, slammed on his brakes and then stuck up his middle finger at me. Boy! I was mad! I got so angry I put my foot on the gas pedal and sped to catch up with him. The Holy Ghost then convicted me and said, "What are you going to do when you get up there? You're the preacher!" After that admonition, I slowly eased my foot off the gas.

I was having prayer at five o'clock every morning. I read my bible daily. I thought I was ready to go and be with the Lord. Yet, God showed me He has to continuously work in me. As people of God, there are some things that will come up in our lives to beset us and throw us off course. We must be watchful and wise and seek after God's righteousness. If we become content and think we don't have to apply the word of God to our lives every day, the flesh will grow and we'll find ourselves responding outside of the will of God.

As I stated, I am an old fashion preacher. I believe the gospel is the power of God unto salvation (Romans 1:16). It can deliver quickly. That's why you may see people who get saved are instantly delivered from smoking and instantly delivered from drinking. The word of God is quick and powerful (Hebrews 4:12). It breaks habits. It sets people free immediately! The Word of God is a deliverer.

Where we mess up is once we experience a transformation and deliverance of God's power, we think that we are ready to preach, and we are ready to teach. However, that's not how it works. You have to learn how to please God. Holiness is that process. It's a way of life.

Our positions, talents or wealth do not automatically qualify us to preach the gospel. Those attributes do not make us suitable teachers of how to live holy. You have to learn how to grow and develop and walk before God.

In many places, people are watering down God's message. We see them with large followings teaching erroneous doctrine, which means a massive number of people are being misled at one time. Those of us who have sat down and learned of God can tell that something is wrong; that something is missing.

People are drifting because we do not want to hurt their feelings. We distort the Word of God to avoid controversy. But as carriers of God's Word, we are responsible for delivering God's message. We do not set out to offend, but if the Word of God offends some folk then we stand by the Word. When we speak, we speak the message, the testimonies, and the standard of God.

Chapter 10: Count up the Cost

In 1963, I took over my father-in-law's church. The church was growing and God gave me a vision to add an education wing onto the old New Community building, I did not know how I was going to do it. I went to school for Math. So, first, I studied the cost of what it would take to build it. I knew how to read blueprints so I hired an architect to draw up the plans for me. I understood how it would look so I told the saints we were going to build the expansion ourselves. I had never built anything before but it was our only option.

I remember my wife's aunt came up to me and said, "I don't know why I'm giving you my money to throw away." We laughed together. But the saints started bringing their money and their skills. And we started to build. The people donated cement and their time, and we laid the foundation. The city inspector came out and approved it. We poured the foundation.

One of the brothers in the church was trying to be a plumber. So, he came by and helped us with the plumbing. We were then ready to build the wall. When the guy who sold me the blocks found out I knew nothing about building, he told me, "Man that building is going fall." I purchased the blocks anyway and Deacon Norman Branch, who was eighty years old at the time, and I started laying them to build the wall. At that time, I didn't know about using a line to level the blocks so by the time I was done with one row, it looked like a snake.

We had gotten about sixty feet when a drunk man came from around the corner staggering. He came up, pointed and said, "Look at that snake…" He told me, "Give me some string!" He re-laid the blocks for that row and came back the next day to lay the blocks to complete that wall. By the time he finished working, I had learned how to lay blocks by watching Him. Deacon Branch and I completed the remaining walls. My Pastor's Aide President's brother was a brick layer, so he brick veneered the building. We built the whole thing and it lasted until we tore it down years later to make room for our new sanctuary. The man who sold us the blocks came by to see it and shook his head in amazement. Everything we needed God provided.

God gives ideas that are greater than we are. He knows we cannot accomplish them without his help. Whenever He gave me the idea, I did not always have the money to do it, but I knew where I wanted to go. I wrote out a plan and counted how much it would cost to complete what God had given me.

Don't start buildings before considering the hidden cost. But don't let the figure stop you from doing what God told you to do. Things fall in line when we depend on the Lord.

God blessed New Community to have a printing ministry. It did not start off as a printing ministry but

God added to it. I purchased an A.B. Dick printing press after I noticed how the church spent a lot of money on printing publications, brochures, newsletters, and tracks. One day, I went to the print shop and I observed how the printer operated the printing press. I watched him for a while then said to myself I can do that. I went and bought an A.B. Dick Printing Press. I purchased all the equipment that was needed and had them assembled in a room in the church. It was about fifteen to twenty thousand dollars' worth of equipment but I knew it would save the church money over time.

I got commitments from four young ladies who were members of the church who agreed to learn how to run the press. When I told my wife my plan, she told me "those girls are not going to want to get their hands dirty." She taught Business Education at Chesapeake Public School, so she worked with the mimeograph press all the time. She would get black ink on her hands and clothes while making copies with the press. She said they would not do it but I was convinced the young ladies would follow through on their commitment. After, the salesmen taught the young ladies how to use the press, they saw how messy it got. So, they backed out of their agreement. They never touched the equipment. It sat there for about a month. Then, I taught myself how to operate it. Deacon Martin Benns, a faithful deacon, stayed with me and we learned how to operate the press. We figured out how to use the equipment because I had a wife in my ear telling me, "I told you so."

After a while, when other churches found out we had a printing press, they began to use us to print their materials for seminars, workshops and events. I did not see our success happening in the beginning but God had it planned for us in the end. He allowed this small idea to transition into a print ministry.

I eventually purchased a camera and learned how to transfer the images onto the plate for the press. I took pictures of all our church events. I was the pastor but I also served as the church photographer. During that time, there were not many black photographers and the camera instructions were written for taking pictures of whites but not of blacks. Whenever I took pictures of blacks the pictures came out too dark. I went to some buddies of mine who were white photographers but no one could figure out why. So, I had to learn.

One day, I opened the lens to snap the picture and the picture came out perfectly. I learned white reflects and dark absorbs. Then I realized the reason blacks were sought after to pick cotton in the early development of our country, was because whites would get skin cancer by being exposed to the sun too long.

Afterwards, the news got out in the community about our distinguished printing services, until someone wanted to partner with us on a government contract. But I declined. Whenever conducting business you must not only look at what it is going to cost you in finance but also in time, and reputation. And some deals I had to walk away from because it would have taken up too much time or ruined our name.

Every idea God gives you will not always start out easy. It may not run smoothly. Situations in life will not always work out perfectly. Others may agree to support you but you may end up working on it alone. You cannot standby and do nothing. Sometimes you may have to do the work yourself.

I will share with you words Bishop Eaton, a close friend of mine, spoke to me in a sermon, after God had given me the vision to build a new church. As I sat in my chair, once again wondering how we were going to build a bigger edifice, Bishop Eaton turned around to me and said, "Bishop Thomas the Lord told me to tell you, you will not see all the money you need all at once, but as you finish one project, another door will be opened." God performed His word. And we built the first phase of our project debt free. After you have counted up the cost, as you move, God will bless you.

I sought the Lord first and He has blessed me tremendously but all He has provided is secondary to who He is in my life.

Bishop Ted G. Thomas Sr.

**St. Stephen's Church of God in Christ
Virginia Beach, VA**

Never Forsaken

**New Community Temple Church of God in Christ
Portsmouth, VA**

CONCLUSION

In Mark 11:11-24, Jesus used the story of the fig tree to teach His disciples a lesson on faith. Jesus made a triumphant entry into Jerusalem; He was hungry and saw a fig tree and desired to eat from it. The tree looked like it had figs. However, it only had leaves. Jesus cursed the tree and told it, it shall not bear anymore fruit. On the next day, Peter noticed the tree was cursed. He said, Master behold the tree that you curse. Peter was amazed that the tree withered away from the root. The miracle in this story was that the tree died overnight. A tree does not die overnight; it takes years. But in this story, this tree dried up from its root overnight. Jesus responded, "Have faith in God."

I also leave these words with you, "Have faith in God."

We have authority with God through Jesus' name.

When we needed the funds to build the addition, my lawyer knew the president of the bank. He told me to use his name. When I went to the bank and used the lawyer's name that gave me an edge. Every believer has the authority to go to God and use Jesus' name and whatever we ask in His name, we can have it. Have faith and only believe.

This book has chronicled some of the stories of my life but it only briefly summarizes some of the manifestations God has performed in my life. As long as I live, I will continue to testify of the goodness of the Lord. I have learned that everything that we could ever pursue on earth will pass; it will perish. If your foundation is not solid you will easily be moved.

As I close, I leave you with these pearls of wisdom: Focus on the word of God. Get to know God. Walk with Him. Learn His ways. Draw close to God and He will tell you some of His secrets. Face your challenges through God; don't run away from them. Don't compromise your standards. Holiness and the word of God are right any day of the week. Be a good steward over what God has placed in your hands and He will multiply it. Be opened to love and you will receive love. Learn to trust one another. Lastly, always seek first the Kingdom of God and His righteousness and the material things you desire will be added to you. Always, throughout your entire life, put God first. Love Him with all your heart and keep Him as the center of your life.

As I close the chapters of this book, I leave you with a few of my sermons to use during your study time. Take some time to look over them and search the scriptures for yourself and God will give you understanding and direction. Be blessed.

Never Forsaken

Bishop Ted G. Thomas Sr.

SERMONS

Never Forsaken

THE CHALLENGE TO OVERCOME DISCOURAGEMENT

Text: 1 King 19:1-4, (4). But he went a day's journey into the wilderness, and came and sat down under a juniper-tree: and he requested for himself that he might die; and said, It is enough; now, O Lord, take away my life; for I am not better than my fathers.

Discouragement is one of the greatest and most effective weapons that the devil has in His arsenal of weapons. In his arsenal, he has trials, tribulation, distress, persecution, famines, disappointments, death, lying, backbiting, etc. and he does not mind using them on the saint. We can so easily become discouraged to the point that we will give up. Church members have become discouraged and leave the church. Mothers have become so discouraged because of the vicissitudes of life, they load their children in the car, only to destroy them all. Husbands have become so discouraged until they tell

Never Forsaken

their wives that they're going to the 711 store, to get a loaf of bread, and never return.

Everyone will have their share of discouragement, at some point and time, on this journey call life. However, for those of us who have been twice born, our approach to managing our discouragements will distinguish us from those who has not yet accepted Jesus Christ, as their Lord and Savior. For we who are twice-born, have the privilege of casting all our cares upon him for He cares for you.

The reason Discouragement is so effective is because it has to do with our emotions: It is defined to be "a feeling of despair and hopelessness in the face of trials and tribulations or obstacles; It bring in a state of great misery and distress, distraught and loss of sense of enthusiasm, loss of drive and courage."
It does not matter who you are or what position you may hold, or your status in life, for discouragement happens in all areas of life. <u>Rick **Warren** said,</u>

Bishop Ted G. Thomas Sr.

"Discouragement is a disease unique to human beings, and it is universal – eventually everyone gets it, including those of us who are in ministry."

A stale marriage. A chronic health condition. A prolonged period of unemployment. Discouragement sets in when you start to feel a sense of hopelessness about your future – when it seems like the troubling circumstances, that you're going through, won't ever get better. But if you look beyond your circumstances and see Jesus, you'll discover the real hope and a better future, lies within the promises of God. You see, it's all in how you manage your discouragements. For those of us who have been twice born deals with discouragement differently than those who have not yet accepted Christ Jesus as their Lord and Savior. The devil will make them think that there is no one to turn to, some people become so discouraged, and distressed out, until they attempt to take their own lives. Such was the case of Elijah.

The prophet Elijah had drifted so far, until he lost focus of who he was and whose he was. He was in a place spiritually where he had no business. He possessed the signs of Discouragement:

Some of the signs of discouragement are:
- His mind and soul were full of worry.
- Absent-mindedness sets in and weariness results.
- Complacency—Loss of interest in food even though you might not have eaten for hours.
- Negative thoughts — The ultimate of these are thoughts of suicide.

Let us briefly consider Elijah's powerful anointing:
1. He was a man of like passion as we are.
2. He earnestly prayed and stopped the dew and rain from flowing for 3 ½ years.
3. He was fed by the ravens and drink from the brook.

4. He blessed the widow's meal barrel, and it never wasted.

5. He could pray down "fire from heaven" set the altar on fire with water.

6. He prayed again and brought a cloudburst down.

But here he is now retreating in weariness, exhaustion, and depression.

ELIJAH LOST HIS "CONFIDENCE, he Lost ASSURANCES in the PROMISES of God." He doesn't look like the "same Elijah" who faced King Ahab and wicked Jezebel. We don't see the faith that he had to "wait daily on the ravens to bring him meat and bread in the morning and meat and bread in the evening. We don't see him displaying the courage that was necessary to stand against the compromising prophets of Baal.

Here we have a discouraged prophet; but let me tell you that prophets and preachers, Missionaries are human beings and can sometimes become the target of depression.

ELIJAH'S CONDITION WAS ADDRESSED AND ANALYZED BY GOD. You don't have to worry, God already knows all about you troubles. The Psalmist asked the question, (Psalm 139:7-12)

7. "Whither shall I go from Thy spirit? Or whither shall I flee from Thy presence?"

8.) If I ascend up into heaven, thou art there: if I make my bed in hell, behold, thou art there.

9.) If I take the wings of the morning and dwell in the uttermost parts of the sea;

10.) Even there shall thy hand lead me, and thy right hand shall hold me.

Elijah began to flee for his life until he became exhausted and flopped down under a juniper tree and goes to sleep. Have you ever felt so down and out, that all that you could do, was go find some place and just lie down?

Bishop Ted G. Thomas Sr.

Have you ever felt that your laboring was fruitless and useless and all in vain? The songwriter said, "sometimes I feel discourage and think my work's in vain, But the Holy Spirit come and revive my soul again." God sent an angel and touch Elijah. Let me assure you, that God sees us, when we are discouraged and despondent and has, a legion of ministering angels, to send, to our rescue. He already knows all about you circumstance.

WHILE WE SEE GOD PROVIDING FOR HIS PROPHET; WE HEAR HIS QUESTION TO ELIJAH IN VERSE 9. "What doest thou here, Elijah?" In other words, why are you out of your anointing? FIRST, HE SENT AN ANGEL TO "FEED ELIJAH," to take care of personal needs. AND THEN HE "SPEAKS AND REBUKES HIM." In his fearfulness, it may have been convenient for him to Retreat to the cave or linger under the juniper tree. But Elijah was trembling in fear when he should have been trusting God, He was pouting, when he should have been praising God.

ELIJAH'S WORK HAD BEEN SUCCESSFUL, YET IT WAS NOT COMPLETE. GOD had to bring ELIJAH "BACK FROM FEAR AND DEPRESSION" TO HIS anointing OF "COURAGE AND VICTORY." God re-commissioned Elijah to leave the cave and "go forth and stand on the mount." God told him to "get up" and "get moving"; there is yet work to be done.

He wants to do the same for you today. Are you "out of your anointing?" Are you being defeated by fear and depression, when you should be building up His Kingdom?

Have you lost that zeal to work for the Lord that you had when you first received him? Are you overwhelmed by the problems of this world? Have you "any rivers that seem uncrossable, have you any mountains that you can't tunnel through?" I can tell you today that God "specializes in things that seem impossible." And he can do what no other power can do. So just turn it over to Jesus and let him work it out. He knows how to work it out. He is waiting to work it out.

Bishop Ted G. Thomas Sr.

We must believe that "the Lord knoweth how to deliver the godly out of temptations" (II Peter 2:9). God can't use us when our anointing has departed from us, and we are "out of our element."

ELIJAH was not a sinful and wicked man; But God rebuked him because he had become unusable. He had not become a drunkard, like Noah, nor a murderer, like Cain. His hands were not stained with blood like those of David; however, he was "out of his anointing" and useless as a prophet.

Every child of God, must strive and do the Will of God, despite the 'caves' of doubt, despite the 'juniper trees' of defeat, which will entice you to lodge in them. **It is a place, that is "off limits" to every Child of God, because it takes us "out of our anointing."** I hear the bible say (I Corinthians 15:58) **"Therefore, my beloved brethren, be ye steadfast, unmovable, always abounding in the work of the Lord, forasmuch as ye know that your labor is not in vain in the Lord.**

Every now and then, we need TO LOOK BACK to SEE where the lord has brought us from, and WHICH DIRECTION WE ARE TRAVELING on this road call LIFE.

Are you safely, walking in the center of God's will? Are you standing on "holy ground?" Sometimes, the way, will get dark and dreary, the load will get hard to bare. Just remember that Lord is our helper. And he is able to see you through.

AFTER Jesus went through his AGONY OF GETHSEMANE; GOD SENT AN ANGEL TO MINISTER TO him and He wax strong and made his way to Cross--HE took that heavy cross and started up the rugged slope of Golgotha, and hung there between a sorrowing HEAVEN and a sinning EARTH, and DIED: until the sun, moon, and stars refused to shine. DIED until the earth began to quake, died until the veil in the TEMPLE rent. And when he had completed the work of REDEMPTION, when he had borne HIS humiliation, when he had drunk the last dreg of HIS sorrow, when HE passed through HIS travail, when he DIED and could DIE no more, with HIS garment rolled in blood, He passed clear through the wine press. John said that He bowed HIS head in the locks of his shoulders, and he himself said, "IT IS FINISHED." UNDER THE "Wait OF THE CROSS" HE CRIED OUT, with a loud voice, "WHY HAS THOU FORSAKEN ME?" He overcame the discouraging features of the cross, and He did not quit, He would not come down from the cross, until He had finished His work of redemption, Salvation was complete. The long march is over. The alien has been made a citizen. The child has been brought back from the far country. The lost have been found. The sunken have been lifted. The lost have been brought back into the fold. Thanks be to god. Yes, it's finished! The work is done. The travail is born. The winepress has been trodden. Redemption is complete! Salvation is made perfect! Hebrews 9:12, "But by his own blood he entered in once into the holy place, having obtained eternal redemption for us."

We like Christ can overcome our discouragements. For He said greater is he that is within you than He that in the world. We can encourage our self, in the word of god; (Galatians 6:9) **"And let us not be weary in well doing: for in due season we shall reap if faint not."**

Wait on the Lord: be of good courage, and he shall strengthen thine heart: stand your ground, keep on believing, keep on trusting, and everything will be alright.

"Be not dismayed, whatever betide, God will take, care of you;

Beneath his wings, of love abide, God will take, care of you; If when you're tried, and fail in you trying, your hands, sore and scarred, from the work you've begun, take up your cross; the cross of disappointment, the cross of criticism, the cross of discouragement, take up your cross, and run quickly to meet Him; He'll understand and say well done.

WHO IS ON THE LORD'S SIDE?

Text: Exodus 32:26 "Then Moses stood in the gate of the camp, and said, who is on the Lord's side? Let him come unto me. And all the Sons of Levi gathered themselves together unto him."

We are living in what I refer to- a crazy world; most folks want to have it their way. People today seem to be infected with what I call the "Burger King Syndrome, I can have it my way" Yet, just about everyone will tell you that they are a born again Christian and that they know the Lord. I came to remind you tonight that we cannot have it our way and yet please God.

If you try to do what's right in the sight of God, they will label you as traditional. But if you are willing to condone everything and every kind of lifestyle, then they will label you as a liberal. There was a time when we just couldn't do all the stuff that we do now and yet be saved. I know we use to say that just about everything one did was a sin, but now we don't call anything a sin. I don't know which is worse. The Bible teaches that we should put a difference between holy and unholy, between clean and unclean. The word of God makes it clear that we must choose whose side we are living on. And it is so relevant today that we let the world know the God we serve. We used to say that America is a Christian Nation. Today that's not actually true. For America is made up of Christians, Jewish, Buddhist, Muslim, Hindu etc. As Americans, we are free to worship as we choose. And we are free to believe in no God.

When Joshua was nearing the close of his life, he called all Israel together and put them in remembrance of all that God had done for them, and challenged them to make a choice. **Joshua 24:15 "Choose you this day whom ye will serve; whether the gods which your fathers served that were on the other side of the flood, or the gods of the**

Amorites, in whose land ye dwell: But as for me and my house, we will serve the Lord."
Revelations 3:15-17 God said to the church of the Laodiceans: "I know thou works, that thou art neither cold nor hot: I would thou wert cold or hot." 16. "So then because thou art lukewarm, and neither cold nor hot, I will spue thee out of my mouth."

It is clear that God is calling us to make a decision. We cannot have it both ways. God has always demanded that we should serve him and him only, **for the supreme commandment says thou shall not have no other god before me**. So today, I want to ask you an important question, namely, **whose side are you living on?**

May God grant us grace to give an honest answer? There are some questions you can't avoid. You'll really have to give an answer or remain silent. And if you remain silent it will be against you. Who is not for us is against us. God grant that we can give an honest answer. And let it be yes. Lord thou knoweth all things. **Now, before I enlarge upon this exceedingly personal and practical question, I must ask you to remember the man who asks this question.** It was Moses who put this question before the people. Who is on the Lord's side? He put it to Israel, the people he had led out of Egypt, when sin was running rampant in the camp. It is well to remember that he stood there a lone man. And let me tell you - that people can backslide (miss the mark) so quickly. Moses had been called by God to meet Him on The Top of Mount Sinai. **And for forty days Moses stood up there in serenity, with the majestic display of God's infallible Glory.** I have had the pleasure of going to Israel twice. But I did not get the opportunity to go up to the top of Sinai. I would have loved to have stood where Moses stood and talk to God. There are 3800 steps to the top of Mt Sinai. It was there that Moses stood in the present of God.

Bishop Ted G. Thomas Sr.

There he stood as a lone man, and remember he had been up there for forty days and in forty days' time the church backslide, and they didn't backslide outside of the Church, they backslide in the church. When he came back down the mountainside, he saw them dancing. **You can be dancing and still backslide.** Moses had under his arms the table of stones with God's Law and commandments on them. And they were dancing and shouting. <u>They were the first topless and nude dancers on record. For they were dancing with their clothes off.</u> For the Bible says. The people were naked, (for Aaron had made them naked unto their shame among their enemies :) They were dancing around a golden calf and telling a lie while they dance.

Dancing does not mean anything, if you don't have the victory. They were saying this is the god that brought us out of Egypt. What a lie. You see when you backslide, you start telling lies. Because you got to lie to cover for you self, to try to make up for what you don't have. I can almost tell when folk start getting weak because they start fussing in their testimonies.

But Moses came down as a Champion. We don't need leaders in this day and time that are weak kneed and spineless. For we must be able defend the cause for which we represent. Unless you can stand and stem the tide, and keep people from going into apostasy and drifting back into the darkness of sin and into the bankruptcy of their character, then we have forfeited our position as leaders. That's why Moses stood a solitary Champaign of Jehovah, and challenged the hold nation to decide for God. **Who's on the Lord side? I see you out here dancing; but everybody that's dancing is not on God's side.** Jesus talked about two men who went to pray. **Everybody that's praying is not on the Lord's side**. (These two men went into the temple to pray and one of the men felt that he was more qualified to pray than the other man. **He was sophisticated and**

conceded in his heart, he felt that he was better than the other man. (He thought that he was better prepared to pray than the other fellow.) And that's what disqualified this man. He said I fast twice a week, which is all right, I don't steal and I don't lie, I pay my tithes, and all of that is well and good. But when he started comparing himself to other folks, he got into trouble with God. Because no one knows what's in any body heart. Man looks at the outward appearance but God looks at the heart. We look at people who look deep. Everybody that looks deep is not deep.

`All of them had backslide; the assistant pastor, the church Mother and the whole bunch had backslid. Dancing around a golden calf. Let me tell you- **people will do more for wrong than they will for right.** You remember Jim Jones, don't you? They gave their homes, they sold their houses, they gave him all their money, and then some of them gave their lives to a rotten stinging lie. They were addicted to a lie. They wouldn't believe the truth. Just like some folk do. They will not support their own home church, yet they send their tithes to the TV preacher, to somebody you have never seen, and they are still giving that one dollar at home. That didn't just start yesterday; it started back in Moses time. Because they did more for Aaron than they did for Moses. They took their golden ear rings off, their bracelets, and their necklaces, all their gold and turn it in to Aaron the assistant pastor who made it into a golden calf.

When Moses came down from the mountain, he was Indignant. Let me tell you something, any leader that's worth his weight, will get angry sometimes. If you are afraid to get indignant and if you are going to swallow everything, and like everything that the people do- then you are in the wrong position. **There are somethings God does not take from us when we get saved.** Some people think holiness is what it is not. Holiness is not a denomination. Holiness is a life style. Holiness does not deprive you of something you must have. Holiness does not take your sex drive form you. But it gives you power to have your own wife and leave the other man's wife along. For the bible says let every man have his own wife. And marriage is honorable and the bed undefiled. Holiness does not take your temple from you, but it gives you the power to be angry and sin not. It's not much to anybody that swallows everything that everyone does, and like everything that everybody is doing. I will have to tell you the truth; **I don't like everything that some people do. And I don't have to like it to be saved.** There are some things God himself don't like. He named seven of them and the first one was a lying tongue. Even a liar doesn't like a liar. I have never seen a liar yet that wants you to tell him a lie.

Moses had to face that crowd. A crowd that had miss the mark. And they were still in church. Apostasy is worse than backsliding, and that is a great strategy that the devil uses on the saints today. You take forty or fifty years ago, the devil thing was to try to get you backslide out of the church. But the devil has change that strategy altogether. Now, he gets us to miss the mark and stay in the church. He is infiltrating every department of the Church. And he has even transformed himself. He doesn't look like the devil. He has attired himself so he will look just like the saints. **As an angle of light**, he has infiltrated the whole thing. They creep in unaware. Let me tell you, it's hard to get them out. For they have influence among the people. That's why Jesus said let the wheat and tares grow together and on the day of Harvest I will do the separating. But Moses said who is on the Lord's side.

We have come to a place in our Christian Walk that we have got to have a show down her. We have got to draw the line. When I was a young boy, and we got ready to fight, we use to draw a line on the ground and dare your opponent to cross that line. But now it's different today, you better not stoop down to draw a line, because if you do you may not get back up. We use to put a chip on each other shoulder and dare the other to knock it off. Today you better leave that chip alone because if you stoop down to get a chip, you may not be able to get up.

But Moses had to stand there as a lone champing and make a whole nation decide. His own brother had practically deceived him, because he had become the means of making the golden calf. The Seventy Elders, who should have been on his side, however, none of them, were present with him. Nobody but his lieutenant Joshua. He stood alone in the midst of the multitude, when they were intoxicated with their lustful pleasures and their fanatical worship. That's what we have got to watch today. You see everybody is making noise today. And we have got to be able to determine whether its true worship or just noise.

Moses was equal to the emergency. We need leaders today that are equal to the times in which we live. We live in a day of issues that must be met. We can't just sit around her, and have good time shouting and dancing and by pass the issues that Young people are facing today. Promiscuity, Promiscuous sex, Pre-marital Sex, Extra marital sex, pornography, abortions same sex marriage and such the like. All of these problem, our young folks are facing, and we have got to say something, we cannot afford to keep silent. For we have got to let them know what side we are standing on because they must decide whose side they are going to stand on.   The world is saying that it is all right; it's an ok situation ethic. Is all right to shake up, (living together without marriage) as long as you are in love with each other? Society says you need to live together before marriage to see if you are compatible. They need to know that there are other alternative life styles. All of these philosophies have come into the main stream of our society. And our young people have to mangle with them. So, they have got to be able to go back with answers that are radically and dogmatically and absolutely true. They must come from our convocations, our pulpits, our conventions and our organizations.

Moses was brave. He knocked down the idol. He took a hammer and ax and broke the idol up into little pieces and burned it and put the ashes in the water and made them drink it. That's the way we use to do. We used to have to drink it. One could not do like many do today. Now one can go off and do wrong then come back and go to shouting and dancing. We used to have to come back and confess our wrongdoing. For the Bible says, if we confess our faults, He would be just and willing to forgive us of our faults.

Moses made them drink it. Moses was daring and brave, he looked them face to face, eye ball to eye ball, He didn't bow down or try act like he was humble, but he stood about them as a man seeking their integrity, seeking their good, seeking to better their character. We are not here to try to be big shots, but we are here representing God's calling. And we have got to do it with courage. It takes courage to be a good leader. I admire the courage of Moses. For he had power. You may ask where he got this power from. Well let me tell you how he got it, for forty days and forty nights Moses had been in the presence of God. Forty days he left the grumbling, vacillating, fluctuating crowd, and was alone in the presence of God. I dare you to get away from folks. I dare you to consecrate yourself. When you get along in the solemnity and the majestic splendor of the presence of God. When you come out, you cannot be the same, something will happen to you. Moses stayed there so long until his countenance change, after forty days and forty nights, in the burning pavilion with God Jehovah. He got so excited until he talked out of turn. His hair stood on its ends. His knees smoked together and he could not restrain himself. And I hear him say; Lord I want to see your Glory. He did not know what God was going to do.

Bishop Ted G. Thomas Sr.

Let me tell you when you get in the spirit it make you adventurous. You get tired of the status Quo. You get tired of the same oh same oh. You want to go higher in God. So, Moses said "Lord show me your Glory." I have been here forty days and forty nights, and I am trimming with adoration, my spirit has over whelmed me. I want to see your Glory. And God said, wait Moses; you ask for something, that's too big for you. Nobody can see me and live. But I will tell you what I will do. I will compromise with you Moses. There is a place that you can get in, and it's over there in the rock, get in the cliff or the rock and when I passed by I will cover you with my hand and after I passed by I will let you see my back parts.

But what is his back part? Now that is a good question. For God is a great God. He so high you can't go over him. He is so wide that you can't go around him. He is so low, that you can't go under him. So, we must come in at the door. So, what did Moses see? He saw the effect of God's presence.

Never Forsaken

That is what will happen to us today if we hide ourselves in the cliff of that rock, For Jesus is that rock we to can have God's Back parts experience by turning our plates down and fasting and praying, get in Jesus

"My hope is built, on nothing less, than Jesus' blood, and righteousness; I dare not trust, the sweetest frame, But wholly lean on Jesus' Name. On Christ, the solid Rock, I stand; All other ground is sinking sand, All other ground, is sinking sand."

THE MYSTERY OF THE INCARNATION OF CHRIST

St. John 1-5:

1. In the beginning was the Word, and the Word was with God, and the Word was God.

    2.   The same was in the beginning with God.

    3.   All things were made by him; and without him was not anything made that was made.

    4.   In him was life; and the life was the light of men.

    5.   And the light shineth in darkness; and the darkness comprehended it not.

TEXT: St. John 1:14; And the Word was made flesh, and dwelt among us, (and we beheld His glory, the glory as of the only begotten of the Father,) full of grace and truth.

What is an Incarnation? It is a theological term, for the coming of God's Son, into the world as a **human being**.

Yes, Jesus was very much human, just as you and I are

human beings. He had all the Characteristics of a human. He was a **baby, toddler**, He went through childhood, adolescent, teenager, adulthood. However, you will not find the term incarnation, in of itself, in the Bible, nevertheless, it is based on clear references, in the New Testament to Jesus as a person "in the Flesh".

So, the incarnation is the act of the embodiment of a spirit in human form. To be giving a human body. (Romans 8:3) For "what the law could not do, in that it was weak through the flesh, God sending his own Son, in the likeness of sinful flesh, and for sin, condemned sin in the flesh:

The marvelous thing about the Incarnation is that: in Jesus, God Himself, lived a full human life, here on earth. Hebrews 5:14. For <u>we have not a high priest which cannot be touched with the feeling of our infirmities; but was in all points tempted like as we are, yet without sin</u>. Jesus' capacity to reveal God to us, and to bring salvation to the world, depended upon His being fully God, and fully man, at the same time. (Colossians 2:9) "For in him dwelleth all the fullness of the Godhead bodily."

<u>The incarnation then</u>, is the Doctrine that the Son of God, was Conceived, in the womb of the Virgin Mary, and, that Jesus is true God, and true man. In other words - <u>Christ was both human and divine.</u> This is the most important doctrine of our New Testament faith (because God was In Christ, Reconciling the world back to himself). For without it, man would still be in his sin, and we, as Paul puts it, are, of all men, most miserable.

> 1Cor. 15:19. *If in this life only we have hope in Christ, we are, of all men, most miserable.*

The human mind, cannot understand, how Jesus can be both fully God, and Fully man, at the same time, *this is why we must accept it by faith.* Without faith, it is impossible to please God.

The Incarnation is a mystery that is hidden from the wise and the powerful, and revealed to babes. (*This is why one must have that simple childlike faith, to accept the plan of salvation)*

Men have spent a lot of time, discussing Mary's Virginity and Joseph's impotence. But the mystery, of the Incarnation is not there. Now, if you look at the whole

spectra of creation, you'll find that God made the first Adam, without a man or a woman.

For in Genesis 1:26 **"And God said, Let us make man in our image, after our likeness..."** In Genesis 1:27, **"So God created man, in his own image, in the image of God, created he him; male and female, created he them."**

This was God's blueprint for man. Notice with me, if you will, <u>if we are created in the image of God</u>, we are created a Spirit. (St. John 4:24, God is a spirit, and they that worship him must worship him in spirit and in truth). But in Genesis 2:7*)* **"And the Lord God formed man of the dust of the ground, and**

Bishop Ted G. Thomas Sr.

breathed into his nostrils the breath of life; and man became a living soul." So, it should not be a surprise, or unrealistic, for God to be able to make the second Adam without a man.

So, then the mystery of incarnation, is not in the Virgin Birth, because God is Sovereign, and does whatever he chooses to do; if He chose to make the second Adam without a man, that's no great mystery.

Not only did He make the first Adam, without a man or a woman - but then He turned around, and made Eve without a woman. (*For he put Adam to sleep, and took a rib from his side, and made the woman with the rib, and gave her to Adam, for a help meet. Adam said since she is bone of my bone, flesh of my flesh, she shall be called Woman*). <u>When he took that rib out of Adam, he took all the women out of man.</u>

So, the first two (2) creatures on Earth were not born, rather they were created - and the second Adam was not born, He was begotten - *"The only begotten of the Father, full of Grace and Truth."*

So, <u>the real mystery of the Incarnation</u>; what most men miss, is the contemplation, of the cataclysmic, that happened when divinity burst into Time, in Bethlehem of Judea, in a Manger, among the Straw - was not that a virgin conceived, <u>but that God was in Christ, Reconciling the world back to himself.</u>

Yes, peering into that manger, seeing The Little Babe was God. I don't know, if we understand it - But all that God is, and all that God will ever be - was centered into that moment - and placed in the manger - the fullness of the
God Head – the Potentate of Paradise, the Creator of everything - the Rock of our salvation, the true and faithful witness, the lion of the tribe of Judah, that's what was in the manger - God was there, All that God is, and all that God will ever be, was in that manger - I envy the sheep, the goats, and the cows - I

Bishop Ted G. Thomas Sr.

wish I could have been there, when God came as a human being.

John said: In St. John 1:3 --*"All things were made by Him; and without Him, was not anything made that was made."* therefore, in that Manger, was the power, that suspended Himself into nothing and said "let there be" - **He put the prestigious oak tree in the ground. He flung the stars in order, He put the Sun, in its trackless path of ether. God was in Christ Reconciling the world back to himself.** That's the mystery of the Incarnation. That God would center Himself, in a manger, and yet be in Heaven - and all over the World, at the same time.

Can you imagine that God, who is all powerful, who is all knowing, and who is everywhere all the time - Decided that He wanted to burst force in time - and the Holy Ghost, had to take God, who is all powerful, who is all knowing, who is everywhere all the time, and compress him down, into a little seed, and thrust him, into virgin Mary's womb - for the Bible says:

that Mary was overshadowed, with the Holy Ghost. No wonder Mary said in St. Luke 1:46, ***"My soul doth magnify the Lord."*** Because God was in Christ. He was not in the prestigious oak tree that he made. He was not the restless sea, He was not in the Stars, that takes their place of central duty, each night in the heaven - **But God was in Christ**. St. John 14:8, Phillip asked Jesus, to show him the Father. Jesus said: ***Have I been so long time with you, and yet hast thou not known me; Philip? He that hath seen me, hath seen the Father.***

St. John 10:30, ***"I and my Father are one."*** Not one in being – Because, Jesus said in St. John 16:28 - "I came forth from the father, and am come into the world: Again, I leave the world, and go to the father."

Not one in the sense of power, St. John 14:28, "**Ye have heard how I said unto you, I go away, and come again unto you - If ye loved me, Ye would rejoice, because I said, I go unto the Father: For**

Bishop Ted G. Thomas Sr.

my father is greater, than I."

Therefore, they are not one in being, they are not one in the sense of personal power, but they are one in purpose, one in plan, one in motive, one in goal, one in purpose for the salvation of mankind. For God was in Christ. That's the mystery of the incarnation:

For my brothers and sisters, the **CENTERPIECE OF OUR CHRISTIAN FAITH, IS THAT GOD WAS IN CHRIST, RECONCILING THE WORLD BACK TO HIMSELF. There are many things the Bible speaks of; it speaks of the glorious nature of God; it speaks of the sovereignty of God, it speaks of meanness and madness of this world, and it speaks of many things. But the centerpiece, of our Christian faith, is that, God was in Christ, bringing the world back, to Himself. That is the living core; that's the vital essence that's the Centerpiece of the NEW TESTAMENT FAITH. GOD was in CHRIST reconciling the world unto HIMSELF.**

For He was the stone, that was hewed out of the mountain, the rose of Sharon, He was that lily of the valley, the bright and morning Star, Wheel in the middle of a wheel, - God was in Christ.

Men have peered, down through the corridors of time, trying to find God. Job said, in Job 23:3, "Oh! that I knew where I might find him! That I might come, even to his seat!" Isaiah said in Isaiah 55:8, "For my thoughts, are not your thoughts, Neither are your ways, my ways." David said in Psalm 55:6, "If I had wings, I'd fly away, to be at rest - Trying to find God."

Isaiah said in Isaiah 6:1, "In the year King Uzziah died, I saw also the Lord, sitting upon a throne, high and lifted up, and His train filled the temple."

So down through the years, men have been searching for God - That's why I envy, the wise men - Because they were the first people, to have seen God - For God

Bishop Ted G. Thomas Sr.

was in Christ.

Why was God in Christ? God was not in Christ, to prove that he could make a Virgin conceive. The Incarnation had **Purpose**; it had **Direction**, and it had **Focus.** God was not in Christ, to impress man, with the miraculous Power - For man's very existence, was a miracle.

But God was in Christ, to bring to man, the Ministry of Reconciliation. For the world, was lost in Sin, and separated from God - The word, reconciliation means, a putting back into adjustment - and God didn't need to be adjusted - because He is the Adjustment of Adjustments - He is the plumb line, by which all other deviations are judged. He didn't need to be changed - He's the changeless one - so if there had to be any adjusting - It was man, who had to be adjusted back to God.

Because of man's fall from grace, sin had messed us up. Sin separated us from God, as a result of Sin, we were alienated, form the Commonwealth of Glory, Sin, blinded us, from the brightness of His Glory. Sin, destroyed our spiritual birthright. Sin, made us outcast, from all the promises of God. Sin, stripped our lives from us, and we became as dead men - Groping in the darkness of sin - So God was in Christ reconciling the world back to Himself. That the very essences--that the very core -- of our New Testament faith -- God was in Christ, reconciling the world, back to Himself.

Sin, is serious business: Do you realize, what sin did to us--God created the world, and everything there in--He then made man, and place him in the garden, with everything he needed. He didn't have to earn his living -- The ground produced spontaneously, all the food he needed -- he didn't have to worry, about anything -- everything he needed, was right there for him. He had face to face fellowship, with God. All he had to do, was obey God's command -- not to eat of the tree of good and evil, -- which was in the midst of the garden. However, man disobeyed God--and sin, came in, and destroyed the relationship, that God had with man.

The man and the woman were both necked, walking around, in the garden. ***It was the first nudist camp on record.*** They were God Conscious and not self-conscious, but when, they disobeyed God, and ate from the tree, which was in the midst of the garden, sin came in:

    1. Man lost that God consciousness and became self-conscious and they knew they were necked

    2. God cursed man: God said by the sweat of your brow ye shall earn your living.

    3. God even cursed the ground, so the ground that once produced spontaneously, began to produce thorn and thistles

    4. And even though man was created--but he said in pain and sorrow - women had to conceive and bare children.

    5. Our bodies began to deteriorate, and

corruption set in--and death entered in because of sin.

Sin, will mess you up. Sin, will make you think you are right, when you are wrong. Sin, will make you think you are up, when you are down. Sin, will make you think you are happy, when you are sad. Sin, will make you think you are well, when you are sick. Sin Destroys: our families, Friendships; Health; Sin, will destroy your mind, sin, will kill you. The devil came to steal kill and to destroy... For the Wages of sin is death, but the gift of God, is eternal Life.

Yes, man was in a mess - we were out of fellowship with God. Nevertheless, God Brooded in His Heart, over the Crown of His Creation - So God, had to get man back. Man couldn't go to God, because of his sinfulness -- God couldn't come to man because of His holiness. So, the only way, to redeem man-- was God had to become man. He had to come where man was - God had to become man without participating in the fall of man, even though, He was identified, with fallen man. God had to become man, without having man's sinful nature. So, God became man, without man's blood. Sinful blood could never bring eternal Life: For Sin corrupts, and brings death. So, God had to become man, and have sinless blood, in order to bring man back to himself - We needed somebody, go man's bond. The search party of angels left heaven to search the world over trying to find some body that was able to go man's bond. They tried Noah, even though God had found favor with Noah, but he couldn't do it, because he drank too much, and got drunk. He tried Abraham, the father of faith. Abraham had disqualified himself by not telling the hold truth. They tried Jacob; he tricked his brother out of his birthright, and his very name meant trickster.

Jesus said prepare me a body and I will go down and go man's bond.

Jesus came down through the 40 &2 Generations, grew and waxed strong, made his way to Cross--*HE took that heavy cross and started up the rugged slope of Golgotha, and hung there between a sorrowing*

HEAVEN and a sinning EARTH and DIED: until the sun, moon, and stars refuse to shine. DIED until the earth began to quake, died until the veil in the TEMPLE rent. And when he had completed the work of REDEMPTION, when he had borne HIS humiliation, when he had drunk the last dreg of HIS sorrow, when HE passed through HIS travail, when he DIED and could DIE no more. With HIS garment rolled in blood, He passed clear through the wine press. John said that He bowed HIS head in the locks of his shoulders, and he himself said as he rested: IT IS FINISHED. THE LONG MARCH IS OVER. THE ALIEN HAS BEEN MADE A CITIZEN. THE CHILD, HAS BEEN BROUGHT BACK, FROM THE FAR COUNTRY. THE LOST, HAS BEEN FOUND. THE SUNKEN HAS BEEN LIFTED. THE LOST HAS BEEN BROUGHT BACK INTO THE FOLD. THANKS BE TO GOD, YES, IT'S FINISHED! THE WORK IS DONE, THE TRAVAIL IS BORN, THE WINEPRESS HAS BEEN TRODDEN, REDEMPTION IS COMPLETE! SALVATION IS MADE PERFECT! Hebrews 9:12, "But by His own blood He entered in once into the holy place, having obtained eternal Redemption for us". "That's why Jesus' Shed Blood, Had So much power."

It redeemed us, it drew us nigh unto him. It made sons and daughters and He became our Father and made Jesus our elderly brother.

I am so glad, that God was in Christ; bringing the world back to himself. Through the precious Blood of Jesus, "what can wash away my sin? Nothing but the Blood of Jesus.
What can make me whole again? Nothing but the Blood of Jesus. O! Precious is the flow, that makes me white as snow; No other fount I know, Nothing but the blood of Jesus."

This is why, I put my trust, and all my hope, in Jesus: He is the one, that died for me, He is the one that set me free, from all my sins .... My hope is built on nothing less than Jesus' blood and righteousness; I dare not trust the sweetest frame, but wholly lean on Jesus' name. On Christ, the solid rock, I stand; all other

Never Forsaken

ground is sinking sand, all other ground is sinking sand.

Bishop Ted G. Thomas Sr.

About the Author

Never Forsaken

Bishop Ted G. Thomas, Sr., B.S., M.A., D.D.
Clergyman-Educator-Entrepreneur; A Biographical Outline

Born:
- October 19, 1935 in Raeford, North Carolina

Family Background:
- Parents: The late Elder Simuel and Mother Nancy Thomas
- Married to Mother Charletta Virginia Clifton Thomas
- Father of six (6) sons: Ted Jr., Christopher (Katrina), Marc Sr. (Naomi), Charles Sr. (Kim), Jonathan and Reuben
- Grandfather of ten (10) grandchildren: JaMerron, Charles Jr., Marc Jr., Emmanuel, Kiara, Evan, Aaron, Ted, Na'ami and Marson

Education:
- Graduate, Norfolk State University, Bachelors of Science Degree in Mathematics
- Graduate, Hampton University, Masters of Science Degree in Mathematics
- Graduate, Trinity Hall College, Doctorate of Divinity Degree
- Moody Bible Institute, Chicago, Illinois;

Clergyman:
- General Board Member, Church of God in Christ, Inc.

- Justice, National Judiciary Board, Church Of God In Christ, Inc. 2008-2012
- Commissioner of Operations, International Holy Convocation 2009-2012
- Assistant Dean, Episcopal Leadership Academy, Church Of God In Christ, Inc.
- Secretary of the National College of Bishops, Church of God in Christ, 1984 -2004
- Prelate, Historic Virginia First Ecclesiastical Jurisdiction, COGIC, Inc., 1984 -present
- Pastor, St. Stephen's COGIC, Virginia Beach, VA, 1991 - present
- Pastor, New Community Temple COGIC, Portsmouth, VA, 1967 - present
- Associate Pastor, Clifton's Tabernacle COGIC, Norfolk, VA, 1963 - 66'
- Ordained 1959

Businessman:
- Proprietor: CMC Holdings, LLC, Carver Memorial Cemetery, Suffolk, Virginia
- Member, Publishing Board, Church of God in Christ, Inc., Memphis, Tennessee
- Chairman, Advisory Board, Bank of the Commonwealth, Portsmouth, Virginia 2000-2011
- Vice-Chairman, Regional Advisory Board, The Bank of the Commonwealth, Norfolk, Virginia 2004 to 2011

Bishop Ted G. Thomas Sr.

BIOGRAPHY OF BISHOP TED G. THOMAS, SR.

Ted G. Thomas, Sr. was appointed seventh in succession as prelate of the **Historic First Ecclesiastical Jurisdiction of Virginia of the Church Of God In Christ** in 1984 and has served in this position for more than 30 years. Under his leadership, the Jurisdiction has enjoyed tremendous growth and has gone from 18 churches to more than 50 in only a few short years. From his early beginnings and through the teaching of godly mentors, Bishop Thomas' ministry has been marked by a steadfast belief in holiness as he upholds the doctrines of the Church Of God In Christ.

Noting his loyalty to God and his leadership, Bishop Thomas caught the attention of the Presiding Bishop and General Board of the Church, and in 1984 the Board of Bishops elected him to serve for five consecutive terms (20 years) as its Secretary. During this time, Bishop Thomas was also selected to represent the Church Of God In Christ on the Board of Directors of the Congress of National Black Churches.

In 2009 Bishop Thomas was appointed as an Associate Justice of the National Judiciary Board, where he meets the qualifications of demonstrating mature judgment, proven ability, integrity and thorough knowledge of the Church Of God In Christ. Bishop Thomas was also appointed Assistant Dean of the Presiding Bishop's Episcopal Leadership Academy in 2009. Bishop Thomas has also served as Commissioner of Operations for the International Holy Convocation, member of the National Publishing Board and member of the Committee to renovate the Lelia Mason Home.

Always a strong supporter of his leader, in an unprecedented and historic show of support for the non-profit organization *Save Africa's Children*, Bishop Thomas presented Presiding Bishop Charles E. Blake with $50,000 during his own 25th Silver Anniversary Celebration in 2009.

Presently, Bishop Thomas serves as a General Board Member of the Church of God in Christ. He is the

Bishop Ted G. Thomas Sr.

pastor of both New Community Temple COGIC in Portsmouth, Virginia where he has served for more than 44 years and St. Stephen's COGIC in Virginia Beach where he has served for more than 20 years. He has also served as district superintendent, administrative assistant to his former prelate, state YPWW president and state Sunday school superintendent.

Bishop Thomas is a long-time educator and recognizes the importance of higher education. He received his Bachelor of Science degree in Mathematics from Norfolk State University and his Master of Science degree from Hampton University. After teaching mathematics for three years, his stellar leadership and youth development skills promoted him to an assistant principal position where he served the Norfolk Public School system for 11 years. Bishop Thomas also taught mathematics at the evening college of Norfolk State University.

Knowing his call to Christian ministry, Bishop Thomas was awarded an Honorary Doctorate of Divinity degree from Trinity Hall College and received further study from Moody Bible Institute, Old Dominion University, Virginia Polytechnic and State University and the College of William and Mary.

With godly wisdom and integrity, Bishop Thomas served for more than 20 years on the Advisory Committee for the Bank of the Commonwealth. He served as the Board Chairman of the Cedar Road Branch and Vice-Chairman of the Advisory Board for all 21 branches of the Bank of the Commonwealth. In this capacity, Bishop Thomas was instrumental in assisting other pastors, several of different jurisdictions and reformations, obtain financing for church expansion. He is the co-owner of the Carver Memorial Cemetery in Suffolk, Virginia.

Bishop Thomas resides in Suffolk, Virginia and is married to Mother Charletta Clifton Thomas. To their

Bishop Ted G. Thomas Sr.

union, the Lord has blessed them with six sons, three daughters-in-law and ten grandchildren.

Retrieved from the Historic VA First Ecclesiastical Jurisdiction.

www.ingramcontent.com/pod-product-compliance
Lightning Source LLC
LaVergne TN
LVHW011421080426
835512LV00005B/198